BOSTON COMMON PRESS
Brookline, Massachusetts

1999

Boston Common Press
17 Station Street
Brookline, Massachusetts 02445

ISBN 0-936184-31-0
Library of Congress Cataloging-in-Publication Data
The Editors of *Cook's Illustrated*

How to barbecue and roast on the grill: An illustrated step-by-step guide to preparing ribs, brisket, pulled pork, salmon, turkey, chicken, beef tenderloin, and pork loin./The Editors of *Cook's Illustrated*
1st ed.

Includes 32 recipes and 36 illustrations
ISBN 0-936184-31-0 (hardback): $14.95
I. Cooking. I. Title
1999

Manufactured in the United States of America

Distributed by Boston Common Press, 17 Station Street, Brookline, MA 02445.

Cover and text design: Amy Klee
Recipe development: Elizabeth Germain
Series editor: Jack Bishop

HOW TO BARBECUE & ROAST ON THE GRILL

An illustrated step-by-step guide to
preparing ribs, brisket, pulled pork,
salmon, turkey, chicken, beef
tenderloin, and pork loin.

THE COOK'S ILLUSTRATED LIBRARY

Illustrations by John Burgoyne

CONTENTS

CONTENTS

introduction

BARBECUE HAS ALWAYS ENJOYED A REPUTATION for being one of the easiest of the culinary arts. But this is undeserved. Like riding a horse, barbecuing may look easy, but after a few minutes in the saddle, as your mount gallops out of control toward the barn, you suddenly appreciate the value of experience. Skill and knowledge are necessary for good barbecue.

The first step in becoming a skilled outdoor cook is to know the difference between grilling, barbecue, and grill-roasting. Grilling is cooking relatively thin, tender foods over high heat. Barbecue is the art of cooking tough, thick cuts of meat over low heat for a long period to add smoke flavor and to tenderize. Grill-roasting is similar, but the heat is moderate instead of low. This technique works well for whole birds, where grilling is out of the question because it would overcook the exterior before the interior was up to temperature.

Beyond these brief definitions, there is much to know. An amateur cook often produces tough, dried out brisket or pork that is hard to "pull" because it has not been cooked properly. After much testing at *Cook's Illustrated*, we have found that starting brisket or pork butt over a charcoal fire and then finishing it wrapped in aluminum foil in a low oven produces incredibly moist, tender meat, similar to what one might find in a Texas barbecue pit. We even discovered a method for barbecuing a whole salmon, producing a delicious outer crust with a moist, tender interior. You will also learn a great deal about how to use charcoal, how to maintain an even fire, and how to use indirect heat.

We have also published *How to Make a Pie, How to Make an American Layer Cake, How to Stir-Fry, How to Make Ice Cream, How to Make Pizza, How to Make Holiday Desserts, How to Make Pasta Sauces, How to Make Salad, How to Grill, How to Make Simple Fruit Desserts, How to Make Cookie Jar Favorites, How to Cook Holiday Roasts and Birds, How to Make Stew,* and *How to Cook Shrimp and Other Shellfish,* and many other titles in this series will soon be available. To order other books, call us at (800) 611-0759. We also publish *Cook's Illustrated,* a bimonthly publication about American home cooking. For a free trial copy of *Cook's,* call (800) 526-8442.

Christopher P. Kimball
Publisher and Editor
Cook's Illustrated

chapter one

BARBECUE & GRILL-ROASTING BASICS

OST COOKS INTUITIVELY UNDERSTAND how to grill. You build the biggest fire possible and place the food—meat, fish, chicken, or vegetables—right over the coals. Once the food is nicely seared on both sides, it's done. Steaks, chops, and other relatively thin foods can be grilled this way because the interior will be cooked by the time the exterior is nicely browned.

But what about a thick pork roast or brisket? If grilled this way, the exterior will be charred and ashen well before the interior of such a large piece of meat has a chance to cook through. Same thing for a whole chicken or turkey.

The solution is indirect cooking, with the lid down (not up, as in grilling) to trap heat and create a regulated cooking environment much like that of an oven.

While grilling calls for filling the grill with charcoal or lighting all the gas burners, indirect cooking on the grill relies on a smaller fire. The lit coals are banked on one side of the grill, or one of the gas burners is turned off. Foods cooked by indirect heat are placed over the "cool" part of the grill. Since there is no direct heat, the exterior of the food cooks slowly without flare-ups. With the lid on, the heat of the fire is trapped, and it cooks the food slowly and evenly.

Why bother with indirect cooking on the grill when you can roast in the oven? The smoky flavor we associate with ribs or pulled pork comes only from the grill. Even foods that we don't normally consider grilling—a whole turkey or side of salmon—taste better when wood flavor is added to the equation.

There are actually two kinds of indirect cooking that are possible on a covered grill. Barbecuing is the traditional low- and slow-cooking method used with ribs, pulled pork (shredded Boston butt), and brisket. Because the goal is to impart as much smoke flavor as possible, a long cooking time over a relatively low fire is required. Barbecuing also provides ample time for fatty, tough cuts to become more lean and tender.

Although there is much debate among barbecue experts as to the proper cooking temperature, we found in our testing that barbecuing should take place between 250 and 300 degrees. While some chefs and pit masters might argue that ribs are best barbecued at 180 degrees, we found it very difficult to maintain such a low fire. Also, such low temperatures allow bacteria to multiply and increase the risk of food-borne illnesses.

Once the sustained (or average) temperature during the cooking period exceeds 300 degrees, we believe (and most experts concur) that the process becomes grill-roasting, the other method of indirect cooking. The grill setup is the same, there's just more heat.

Grill-roasting is best for foods that are already tender and that don't require low and slow cooking. Birds are especially well suited to grill-roasting (at lower temperatures the skin remains soft and flabby), as are tender cuts of meat (like beef tenderloin) that need to develop a crisp crust during their relatively short cooking time. Grill-roasting occurs between 300 and 400 degrees. (It's hard to sustain much higher temperatures by indirect cooking; for comparison, true grilling occurs at temperatures in excess of 500 degrees.)

Salmon might seem to be an ideal candidate for grill-roasting. Clearly, this fish does not need the long cooking time provided by barbecuing to render fat and become tender. But we found that grill-roasted salmon cooks so quickly that the fish doesn't pick up enough smoke flavor. Thus, we prefer the lower cooking temperature of barbecuing to lengthen the cooking time.

SMOKE

One of the best reasons to barbecue or grill-roast is to flavor foods with smoke. Charcoal itself has some flavor (gas adds none), but the real smoky flavor of good ribs or brisket comes from wood chunks or chips. Chips will work on either a charcoal or gas grill (see the following pages for details), but chunks are suited to charcoal fires only, since they must rest in a pile of lit coals to work. (If placed on the bottom of a gas grill they will not get hot enough to smoke.)

Hickory is the most traditional wood used for outdoor cooking, but there are other choices. In our tests, we found that any hardwood chunks or chips can be used. Frankly, the differences in flavor are minimal, especially if the food has been coated with spices. The difference between hickory and mesquite, for instance, is hard to taste on spice-rubbed ribs but will be more perceptible on a chicken that has been rubbed with butter, salt, and pepper and nothing else. We have noted traditional pairings (such as ribs and hickory or salmon and alder) throughout the book, but feel free to use whatever wood is available.

11

CHARCOAL VERSUS GAS GRILLS

Our preference when grilling is to use charcoal. We like the way it heats up and the flavor that food absorbs from hardwood charcoal (our favorite fuel for most recipes). However, when doing indirect cooking—barbecuing or grill-roasting—many of the advantages that charcoal grills have over gas grills disappear.

Hardwood charcoal, also called natural or lump charcoal, tends to burn too quickly. It's too hot to be practical when cooking by indirect heat. We like the intense fire this charcoal makes when searing steaks, but when using it to barbecue brisket, you have to open the grill and add charcoal much more often than you'd like. Also, because the fire can run hotter at the outset, there is a greater risk of burning the edges of large foods (such as turkeys and ribs) that may be close to the coals. For indirect cooking, we prefer to use regular charcoal briquettes, which burn cooler and more slowly.

Briquettes don't have as much flavor as hardwood charcoal, but they do give foods a more smoky flavor than a gas grill. Whether grilling over briquettes or gas, wood chunks or chips must do the real flavoring work. In our testing, we consistently found that foods cooked over charcoal had a smokier flavor than those cooked over gas. That's because a charcoal fire does a better job of getting the wood (which is

1 2

sitting right in the fire) to smolder and smoke.

Although we eventually devised a method for maximizing the smoke from chips used in a gas grill (*see* page 22), the smoke flavor is not as strong as it is in foods cooked over charcoal. If you like really smoky foods and are using a gas grill, you might consider using more chips at the outset when grill-roasting or adding more chips to the foil tray partway through the cooking time when barbecuing.

Intense smoky flavor aside, gas grills do have some advantages over charcoal when cooking by indirect heat. It's easier to regulate the heat on a gas grill. Just turn the dial and the temperature immediately responds. Also, there is no need to add charcoal during the long cooking process, so there is less hassle and mess. Gas grills are also more convenient to use during rainy weather.

Finally, our tasters felt that foods cooked over gas were juicier than foods cooked over charcoal. The reason for this is simple. Smoke makes foods taste great but causes them to dehydrate. Since gas grilling generates less smoke, foods retain more moisture. That's why we found that brining birds and other foods that tend to dry out is especially important when cooking over charcoal. Brining adds flavor to foods that will be cooked over gas, but it has a less noticeable effect on texture.

In the end, we found that cooking with charcoal or gas

produces excellent, if somewhat different, results. For your convenience, each recipe in this book has been adapted for both types of grilling.

USING A CHARCOAL GRILL FOR INDIRECT COOKING

We find that a kettle-style grill rather than a rectangular hibachi is the best choice when using charcoal. The deep bowl shape allows air to circulate, and the high lid accommodates even tall foods like a turkey. Choose the largest grill possible, preferably one with a grate that measures 22 inches across. On smaller grills, the "cool" part of the grill will be too cramped to accommodate a turkey or two slabs of ribs.

Before starting, empty the grill of any old ashes, which may block air circulation and prolong cooking times when barbecuing or grill-roasting. We find that a flue starter, or chimney starter, is the most efficient way to light charcoal. (*See* figures 1 through 4 for instructions on lighting the charcoal and setting up the grill for indirect cooking.) A chimney starter is foolproof, and it eliminates the need for lighter fluid, which can impart off flavors to delicate foods such as fish and vegetables.

Some experts recommend banking the coals on either side of the grill and leaving the center open for indirect cooking. They believe that having the coals on both sides of the grill promotes even heating. When we tried this method, we found that the edges of large pieces of food, such ribs, brisket, and turkey, can burn. We prefer to bank all the coals on one side of the grill, leaving half of the grill free of coals and providing a large space for foods to cook without danger of burning. Since the lid is down, the heat from the coals is distributed just as well as with two piles of charcoal.

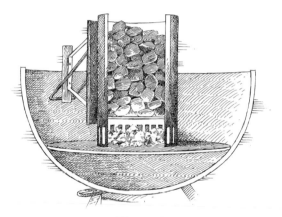

Figure 1.
Fill the bottom section of a chimney starter with crumpled news-paper, set the starter on the bottom grate in a kettle grill, and fill the main compartment with as much charcoal as directed in individual recipes. When you light the newspaper, flames will shoot up through the charcoal, igniting it.

Figure 2.

When the coals are well lit and covered with a layer of gray ash,
dump them onto the charcoal grate, piling the coals up on one half
of the grill and leaving the other half free of coals. If necessary, use
long-handled tongs to move the briquettes into place.

Figure 3.

Place soaked and drained wood chunks or a foil packet filled with
wood chips on top of the coals (see page 18). Set the top grate in
position, heat briefly, and then scrape the grate clean with a wire
brush. You are now ready to cook over the cool part of the fire.

Figure 4.
We like to have some idea of what the temperature is inside a kettle grill as foods cook. A grill thermometer inserted through the vents on the lid can tell you if the fire is too hot or if the fire is getting too cool and it's time to add more charcoal. You can control the heat level to some extent by adjusting the vents on the lid and base of the grill. Opening the vents gives the fire more oxygen and will cause the coals to burn hotter at first, but then the fire will cool down more quickly as the coals peter out. Closing the vents partially (don't close the vents all the way or the fire will die) lowers the heat but keeps the coals from burning up too fast and helps the grill retain heat.

17

WOOD ON A CHARCOAL GRILL

Wood chunks are the easiest way to add smoke flavor when cooking over charcoal. You don't want the wood to catch fire and give up all its smoke at once. Ideally, the chunks should smolder slowly, releasing smoke for as long as possible. We found that soaking chunks adds enough moisture to the wood to prevent it from catching fire as soon as it is placed on the charcoal.

If using wood chunks, soak as many three-inch chunks (each the size of a tennis ball) as directed in each recipe in cold water to cover for one hour. Drain the chunks and place them directly on the lit pile of charcoal.

If you can't find wood chunks, small wood chips may be used. To keep the chips from burning up too quickly, we found it best to wrap them in a foil packet. (There's no need to soak these chips; the foil protects them from catching fire too quickly.) We tried soaking the chips and throwing them directly onto the coals, but they caught fire immediately. The same thing happened when we placed the chips in an open foil tray on top of the coals—an open tray does not provide enough protection for the chips and can tip over if placed on an uneven pile of charcoal.

If using wood chips, follow figures 5 and 6 to wrap chips in heavy-duty aluminum foil. Note that regular foil does not offer enough protection and the chips can catch fire.

18

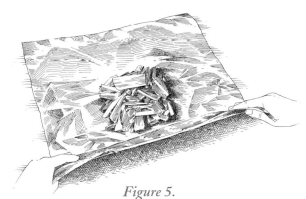

Figure 5.

Place the amount of wood chips called for in the recipe in the center of an 18-inch square of heavy-duty aluminum foil. Fold in all four sides of foil to encase the chips.

Figure 6.

Turn the foil packet over. Tear about six large holes (each the size of a quarter) through the top of the foil packet with a fork to allow smoke to escape. Place the packet, with holes facing up, directly on a pile of lit charcoal.

USING A GAS GRILL FOR INDIRECT COOKING

As with a charcoal grill, size matters when trying to cook certain foods on a gas grill. For instance, the lid must be tall enough to accommodate a turkey resting in a V-rack. (A lid that is less than eight or nine inches tall will be a problem.) Likewise, the size of the cooking grate is important when trying to prepare ribs. Unless the cooking surface has an area of at least 400 square inches, you will need to cook one slab at a time. (If the grill comes with a warming rack, you may cook a second slab there.)

In addition to size, the number of burners is critical. It's not possible to cook indirectly on a grill with only one burner, because the burner is usually positioned in the center of the grill and the "cool" parts of the grill are too small to fit most foods. You must use a grill with at least two burners. With one burner on and one burner off, at least half of the grill will be cool enough for slow cooking.

Just as important, buy a gas grill with a thermometer. You can stick an oven thermometer on the cooking grate, but then you have to open the lid to find out the temperature. Opening the lid causes heat to be lost and prolongs total cooking time. Also try to buy a grill with a gas gauge. Many of the recipes in this book require several hours of cooking, and there's nothing worse than running out of gas unexpectedly.

In our tests, we found it slightly easier to cook on grills with left and right burners rather than front and back. The cooking grate on most gas grills is rectangular. When the grill is divided into front and back cooking zones, the cool part of the grill will be a long, relatively narrow band. Although this shape is well suited to ribs and tenderloin, it can be a challenge when cooking a turkey. When the grill is divided into left and right cooking zones, each side is roughly a square, which we find to be a better shape for cooking birds. Foods that are long and thin, like tenderloin, can be easily curled in a C-shape over the cool side of the grill.

To set up a gas grill for indirect cooking, remove all warming shelves attached to the hood or the back of the grill. (Leave the racks in place when making ribs on a small grill.) Place a foil tray with wood chips (*see* figures 7 through 10) on top of the primary burner (*see* figure 11). With some gas grills, one burner must be turned on first. This is the primary burner. With other grills, you may designate a primary burner yourself. Light all burners and cover the grill. When you see a lot of smoke (this will take about 20 minutes), turn off the burner(s) without the chips and place the food over these off burners. If the chips start to flame, douse the fire with water from a squirt bottle.

WOOD ON A GAS GRILL

Chips are the only choice for gas grills since chunks are hard to position right over a lit burner and may not get hot enough to smoke. We tried various methods for adding chips before we hit upon the best solution.

When we tossed either unsoaked or soaked chips directly into the bottom of a gas grill, they burned much too quickly and gave up all their smoke or did not smoke at all because they fell below the burners. We tried the foil packet method that worked well with charcoal, but found that in this case the packet actually was too effective a shield and not enough smoke was being released.

We prefer to place the chips in an open foil tray. The tray (which can be made from heavy-duty aluminum foil; *see* figures 7 through 10) shields the chips from direct contact with the burner but is open on top to allow the smoke to flow freely. The tray also allows you to spread out the chips so that they are not piled on top of each other, as they are inside a smaller foil packet. More chips can also be added to the tray throughout the cooking process. When we placed unsoaked chips in the tray they caught fire immediately. Soaking the chips for 15 minutes prevents them from igniting and allows them to smolder slowly and produce a lot of smoke.

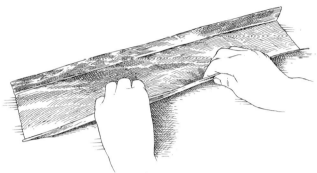

Figure 7.

*Start with a 12- by 18-inch piece of heavy-duty foil. Make a
1 inch fold on one long side. Repeat three more times and turn
the fold up to create a sturdy side that measures about 1 inch
high. Repeat the process on the other long side.*

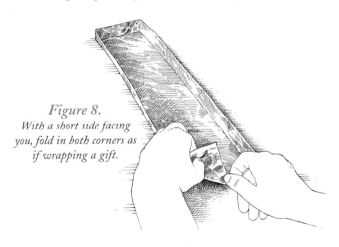

Figure 8.
*With a short side facing
you, fold in both corners as
if wrapping a gift.*

23

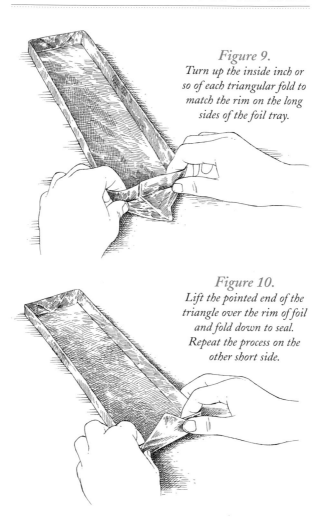

Figure 9.
Turn up the inside inch or
so of each triangular fold to
match the rim on the long
sides of the foil tray.

Figure 10.
Lift the pointed end of the
triangle over the rim of foil
and fold down to seal.
Repeat the process on the
other short side.

Figure 11.
When using a gas grill, place the soaked chips in the foil tray and
set it over the burner you plan to leave on during the cooking
process (in this case the front one—we call this the primary
burner). Make sure the tray is resting securely over the burner
and will not tip. Replace the grill rack and preheat
the grill as directed.

chapter two

BARBECUED RIBS

E WANTED TO KNOW WHETHER IT IS possible to produce "authentic" ribs (the kind you get at a barbecue joint) at home. We started by cooking ribs—for us, this means pork spareribs—three different ways. One slab was cooked over indirect heat, one parboiled and then grilled over direct heat, and the third cooked on a rotisserie attachment to our grill—we were reluctant to use this unusual bit of equipment but, in the name of science, thought we should give it a shot. All three tests were conducted over charcoal with hickory chips in a covered grill.

The ribs cooked over indirect heat were the hands-down favorite. Those cooked on the rotisserie were not nearly as tender, and the parboiled ribs retained the unappealing flavor of boiled meat. While the indirect method needed some refinement, we were convinced it is the best way to cook ribs at home. It also came closest to replicating the method used by barbecue pit masters.

We prefer regular spareribs to either baby back ribs or country-style ribs (*see* figure 12). The latter ribs are leaner, and therefore prone to drying out, but the extra fat on spareribs helps keep the meat tender and moist during the long cooking process.

We tested a number of popular techniques for barbecuing ribs. Some experts swear by placing some source of moisture in the grill, most often an aluminum pan filled with water or beer. We filled a pan with water and put it next to the coals to create some steam. We couldn't taste the difference between ribs cooked with or without the water.

Next, we tested turning and basting. We found that for the even melting of the fat, it is best to turn the ribs every half hour. Turning also ensures even cooking. When turning, work as quickly as possible to conserve heat in the grill; don't leave the lid off and wander away to find a pair of tongs. Basting proved to be a bust. Tomato-based sauces burn over the long cooking time, and we didn't find the meat any moister after basting.

Under normal weather conditions, we found the ribs to be done in two to three hours. Signs of doneness include the meat starting to pull away from the ribs (if you grab one end of an individual rib bone and twist it, the bone will actually turn a bit and separate from the meat) and a distinct rosy glow on the exterior. Since the ribs require a relatively short cooking time, there is no need to replenish the coals. A fire that starts out at 350 degrees will drop back to around 250 degrees by the end of two hours.

At this point in our testing, we had produced good ribs, but they were not quite as moist and tender as some restaurant ribs. We spoke with several pit masters, and they suggested wrapping the ribs when they come off the grill. We wrapped the ribs in foil and then placed them in a brown paper bag to trap any escaping steam. After an hour, we unwrapped the ribs and couldn't believe the difference. The flavor, which was great straight off the grill, was the same, but the texture was markedly improved. The wrapped ribs literally fell off the bone.

We spoke with several food scientists who explained that as the ribs rest, the juices are evenly distributed back through the meat and the resulting ribs are more moist and more tender. In fact, our ribs are so flavorful and tender that we consider sauce optional.

☙

Master Recipe

Barbecued Ribs

➤ **NOTE:** *We prefer regular spareribs (see figure 12) to baby back or country-style ribs, both of which are less fatty and can dry out as they barbecue. Hickory is the traditional wood choice with ribs, but some of our tasters liked mesquite as well. Serves four.*

- 2 full slabs pork spareribs (about 6 pounds total)
- ¾ cup Dry Rub for Barbecue (page 92)
- 2 3-inch wood chunks or 2 cups wood chips
  Heavy-duty aluminum foil
  Brown paper grocery bag
- 2 cups Barbecue Sauce (page 94), optional

■■ INSTRUCTIONS:

1. Rub both sides of ribs with dry rub and let stand at room temperature for 1 hour. (For stronger flavor, wrap rubbed ribs in double layer of plastic and refrigerate for up to one day.)

2. Soak wood chunks in cold water to cover for 1 hour and drain, or place wood chips on 18-inch square of aluminum foil, seal to make packet, and use fork tines to create about six holes to allow smoke to escape (*see* figures 5 and 6, page 19).

3. Meanwhile, light about 40 charcoal briquettes in chimney. Transfer hot coals from chimney to one side of kettle grill, piling them up in a mound two or three briquettes high. Keep bottom vents completely open. When coals are covered with light gray ash, lay wood chunks or packet with chips on top of charcoal. Put cooking grate in place, open grill lid vents completely, and place lid on grill, turning lid so that vents are opposite wood chunks or chips to draw smoke through grill. Let grate heat for 5 minutes, clean with wire brush, and position ribs over cool part of grill. (Initial temperature will be about 350 degrees and will drop to 250 degrees after 2 hours.)

4. Barbecue, turning ribs every 30 minutes, until meat starts to pull away from ribs and has rosy glow on exterior, 2 to 3 hours. Remove ribs from grill and completely wrap each slab in foil. Put foil-wrapped slabs in brown paper bag, and crimp top of bag to seal tightly. Allow to rest at room temperature for 1 hour.

5. Unwrap ribs and brush with barbecue sauce if desired or serve with sauce on side.

▪▪ VARIATION:
Barbecued Ribs on a Gas Grill
If working with a smaller grill, place the second slab of ribs on the warming rack.

Follow Barbecued Ribs Master Recipe, making the following changes: Place foil tray with soaked wood chips (*see* figures 7 through 10, page 23) on top of primary burner (*see* figure 11, page 25). Turn all burners to high and preheat with lid down until chips are smoking heavily, about 20 minutes. Turn primary burner down to medium, turn off burner(s) without chips, and clean grill with wire brush. Position ribs over cool part of grill. Barbecue, turning ribs every 30 minutes, until done, 2 to 3 hours. (Temperature inside grill should be constant 275 degrees; adjust lit burner as necessary.) Wrap, rest, and brush ribs with barbecue sauce.

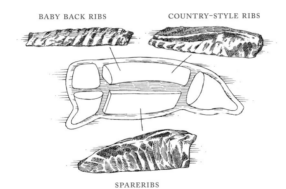

BABY BACK RIBS   COUNTRY-STYLE RIBS

SPARERIBS

Figure 12.

Spareribs come from the side or underbelly of the pig and have the most fat, making them the best choice for barbecuing. Baby back ribs (sometimes called back ribs or loin back ribs) come from the loin (or back) of the pig where the bones are shorter. Country-style ribs are cut from further along the back (closer to the legs). These ribs are quite large and meaty.

31

chapter three

⌇

BARBECUED
BEEF BRISKET

THE MAIN REASON IT'S SO HARD TO COOK brisket right is that it starts out as a very tough cut of meat. Unless brisket is fully cooked, the meat is very chewy and practically inedible. Because a brisket is so large, cooking the meat fully can take many hours. Our goal was to make the meat as tender as possible as quickly as possible.

So what does "fully cooked" mean when talking about brisket? To find out, we roasted four small pieces to various internal temperatures. The pieces cooked to 160 and 180 degrees were dry and quite tough. A piece cooked to 200 degrees was slightly less tough, although quite dry. A final piece cooked to 210 degrees had the most appealing texture and the most pleasant chew, despite the fact that is was the driest.

So what's going on here? Heat causes muscle proteins to uncoil and then bond together, which drives out juices in the same way that wringing removes moisture from a wet cloth. This process starts in earnest at around 140 degrees, and by the time meat reaches 180 degrees most juices have been expelled. This explains why a medium-rare steak (cooked to 130 degrees) is much juicier than a well-done steak (cooked to 160 degrees).

With tender cuts, like steak, the lower the internal temperature of the meat, the juicier and less tough the meat will be. However, with cuts that start out tough, like brisket, another process is also at work. Brisket is loaded with waxy-looking connective tissue called collagen, which makes the meat chewy and tough unless fully cooked. Only when the collagen has been transformed into gelatin will the meat be tender. Collagen begins to convert to gelatin at 150 degrees, but the conversion process occurs most rapidly at temperatures above 180 degrees.

When cooking brisket, the gelatinization of collagen must be the priority. Thus, the meat should be cooked as fully as possible, or to an internal temperature of 210 degrees. The muscle juices will be long gone (that's why the sliced meat is served with barbecue sauce), but the meat will be extremely tender because all the collagen will have been converted to gelatin.

It is important to point out that moist-heat cooking methods (such as braising) are appropriate for cooking meats to such high internal temperatures because water is a more efficient conductor of heat than air. Meats cooked in a moist environment heat up faster and can be held at high internal temperatures without burning or drying out.

Given the fact that brisket must be fully cooked and that the meat is so big (a full brisket can weigh 13 pounds), the meat needs 10 or 12 hours of barbecuing to reach the fork-tender stage. Even when butchers separate the brisket into smaller pieces, as is often the case (*see* figure 13), the cooking time is astronomical. Most cooks are not prepared to keep a fire going that long.

To get around this all-day-long-tending-the-fire problem, we found it necessary to commit barbecue heresy. After much testing, we decided to start the meat on the grill but then finish in the oven, where it could be left to cook unattended. We wondered how long the meat would have to stay on the grill to pick up enough smoke flavor. In our testing, we found that two hours allowed the meat to absorb plenty of smoke flavor and created a dark brown, crusty exterior.

At this point, the meat is ready for the oven. We found it best to wrap the meat in foil to create a moist environment. (Unwrapped briskets cooked up drier, and the exterior was prone to burning.) After barbecuing, a whole brisket requires three hours or so in a 300-degree oven to become fork-tender. Barbecue purists might object to the use of the oven, but this method works and doesn't require a tremendous commitment of hands-on cooking time.

Some further notes about our testing. Although many experts recommend basting a brisket regularly as it cooks on the grill to ensure moistness, we disagree. Taking the lid off wreaked havoc with our charcoal fire, and the meat didn't taste any different despite frequent basting with sauce. Likewise, we don't recommend placing a pan filled with water (we also tried beer) on the grill. Some barbecue masters believe that the liquid adds moisture and flavor to the meat, but we couldn't tell any difference between brisket cooked with and without the pan of liquid.

Brisket comes with a thick layer of fat on one side. We tried turning the brisket at it cooks, thinking this might promote even cooking. However, we had better results when we barbecued the brisket fat side up the entire time. When positioned this way, the fat slowly melts and lubricates the meat below.

Master Recipe

Barbecued Beef Brisket

NOTE: *Cooking a whole brisket, which weighs at least 10 pounds, may seem like overkill. However, the process is easy, and the leftovers keep well in the refrigerator for up to four days. (Leave leftover brisket unsliced, and reheat the foil-wrapped meat in a 300-degree oven until warm.) Don't worry if your brisket is a little larger or smaller; split-second cooking times are not critical since the meat is eaten very well-done. Still, if you don't want to bother with a big piece of meat, barbecuing brisket for less than a crowd is easy to do. Simply ask your butcher for either the point or flat portion of the brisket, which weigh about half as much as the whole brisket. Then follow this recipe, reducing the spice rub by half and barbecuing for just 1½ hours. Wrap the meat tightly in foil and reduce the time in the oven to 2 hours. No matter how large or small a piece you cook, save the juices the meat gives off while in the oven to enrich the barbecue sauce (*see *figure 16). Hickory and mesquite are both traditional wood choices with brisket. Serves 18 to 24.*

- ¾ cup Dry Rub for Barbecue (page 92)
- 1 whole beef brisket (*see* figure 13), 9 to 11 pounds, fat trimmed to ¼-inch thickness
- 2 3-inch wood chunks or 2 cups wood chips
- Heavy-duty aluminum foil
- 2 cups Barbecue Sauce (page 94)

▦ INSTRUCTIONS:

1. Apply rub liberally to all sides of meat, pressing down to make sure spices adhere and completely obscure meat. Wrap tightly in plastic wrap and refrigerate for 2 hours. (For stronger flavor, refrigerate brisket for up to 2 days.)

2. One hour prior to cooking, remove brisket from refrigerator, unwrap, and let come to room temperature. Soak wood chunks in cold water to cover for 1 hour and drain, or place wood chips on 18-inch square of aluminum foil, seal to make packet, and use fork to create about six holes to allow smoke to escape (*see* figures 5 and 6, page 19).

3. Meanwhile, light about 40 charcoal briquettes in chimney. Transfer hot coals from chimney to one side of kettle grill, piling them up in a mound two or three briquettes high. Keep bottom vents completely open. When coals are covered with light gray ash, lay wood chunks or packet with chips on top of charcoal. Put cooking grate in place, open grill lid vents completely and place lid on grill, turning lid so that vents are opposite wood chunks or chips to draw smoke through grill. Let grate heat for 5 minutes, clean with wire brush, and position brisket, fat side up, on grate opposite fire. Barbecue without removing lid for 2 hours. (Initial temperature will be about 350 degrees and will drop to 250 degrees after 2 hours.)

4. Adjust oven rack to middle position and preheat oven to 300 degrees. Attach two 48-inch long pieces of heavy-duty foil by folding long edges together two or three times, crimping tightly to seal well, to form an approximate 48- by 36-inch rectangle. Position brisket lengthwise in center of foil. Bring short edges over brisket and fold down, crimping tightly to seal (*see* figure 14). Repeat with long sides of foil to seal brisket completely (*see* figure 15). Place brisket on jelly roll pan; bake until meat is fork-tender, 3 to 3½ hours.

5. Remove brisket from oven, loosen foil at one end to release steam, and let rest for 30 minutes. If you like, drain juices into large bowl (*see* figure 16) and defat juices in gravy skimmer.

6. Unwrap brisket and place on cutting board. Separate into two sections and carve (*see* figures 17 and 18). Serve with plain barbecue sauce or with barbecue sauce that has been flavored with up to 1 cup of defatted brisket juices.

:: V A R I A T I O N :
Barbecued Beef Brisket on a Gas Grill
Follow Barbecued Beef Brisket Master Recipe, making the following changes: Place foil tray with soaked wood chips (*see* figures 7 through 10, page 23) on top of primary burner (*see* figure 11, page 25). Turn all burners to high and preheat with lid down until chips are smoking heavily, about 20

minutes. Turn primary burner down to medium, turn off burner(s) without chips, and clean grill with wire brush. Position brisket, fat side up, over cool part of grill. Barbecue for 2 hours. (Temperature inside grill should be constant 275 degrees; adjust lit burner as necessary.) Proceed with Master Recipe as directed.

POINT CUT

FLAT END

Figure 13.
Butchers sometimes separate the whole brisket into two parts, the flat end (left portion) and the point cut (right portion). The point cut is a bit thicker and contains more fat. It is more tender than the flat end when barbecued.

39

Figure 14.
After barbecuing, place the brisket on two 4-foot sections of
heavy-duty foil that have been sealed together to make a
4- by 3-foot rectangle. Bring short ends of foil up over the brisket
and crimp tightly to seal.

Figure 15.
Seal the long sides of the foil packet tightly up against the sides
of the meat.

40

Figure 16.
After the brisket comes out of
the oven, use pot holders or
oven mitts to lift the jelly
roll pan and carefully pour
the juices into a bowl.
Reserve the juices and defat
if you like. They make a
delicious addition to the
barbecue sauce.

Figure 17.
Since the grain on
the two sections of
the brisket goes in
opposite directions,
separate the two cuts
before slicing.

Figure 18.
Carve the brisket into
long, thin slices, cutting
against the grain on
the diagonal.

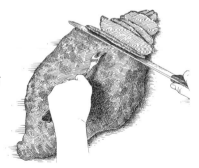

chapter four

§

BARBECUED PULLED PORK

ULLED PORK, ALSO CALLED PULLED PIG OR sometimes just plain barbecue, is slow-cooked pork roast, shredded and seasoned, and then served on a hamburger bun (or sliced white bread) with just enough of your favorite barbecue sauce, a couple of dill pickle chips, and a topping of coleslaw.

Our goal was to devise a procedure for cooking this classic southern dish that was at once both doable and delicious. The meat should be tender, not tough, and moist but not too fatty. Most barbecue restaurants use a special smoker. We wanted to adapt the technique for the grill. We also set out to reduce the hands-on cooking time, which can

4 2

stretch to eight hours of constant fire tending in some recipes.

There are two pork roasts commonly associated with pulled pork sandwiches: the shoulder roast and the fresh ham (*see* figure 19). In their whole state, both are massive roasts, anywhere from 14 to 20 pounds. Because they are so large, most butchers and supermarket meat departments cut both the front and back leg roasts into more manageable sizes: The part of the front leg containing the shoulder blade is usually sold as either a pork shoulder roast or a Boston butt and runs from six to eight pounds. The meat from the upper portion of the front leg is marketed as a picnic roast and runs about the same size. The meat from the rear leg is often segmented into three or four separate boneless roasts called a fresh ham or boneless fresh ham roast.

For barbecue, we find it best to choose a cut of meat with a fair amount of fat, which helps keep the meat moist and succulent during long cooking and adds considerably to the flavor. For this reason, we think the pork shoulder roast, or Boston butt, is the best choice. We found that picnic roasts and fresh hams will also produce excellent results, but they are our second choice.

To set our benchmark for quality, we first cooked a Boston butt using the traditional low-and-slow barbecue method. Using a standard 22-inch kettle grill, we lit about

30 coals and cooked the roast with indirect heat, adding about eight coals every half-hour or so. It took seven hours to cook a seven-pound roast. While the meat was delicious, tending a grill fire for seven hours is not very practical.

In our next test we tried a much bigger initial fire, with about five pounds of charcoal. After the coals were lit, we placed the pork in a small pan and set it on the grate. The trick to this more intense method is not to remove the lid for any reason until the fire is out three hours later. Because you start with so many coals, it is not necessary to add charcoal during the cooking time. Unfortunately, the high initial heat charred the exterior of the roast and the interior was still tough and not nearly "fork-tender" when we took it off the grill.

Next, we tried a combination approach: a moderate amount of charcoal (more than the low-and-slow method but less than the no-peek procedure), cooking the pork roast for three hours on the grill and adding additional coals four times. We then finished the roast in a 325-degree oven for two hours. This method produced almost the same results as the traditional barbecue but in considerably less time and with nine fewer additions of charcoal.

As with ribs (and all barbecue), we find it helpful to let the finished roast rest in a sealed paper bag for an hour. The meat reabsorbs the flavorful juices. In addition, the sealed bag produces a steaming effect that helps break down any remaining tough collagen. The result is a much more savory and succulent roast. Don't omit this step; it's the difference between good pulled pork and great pulled pork.

As with all barbecue, pork roast benefits from being rubbed with a ground spice mixture. However, because the roast is so thick, we find it best to let the rubbed roast "marinate" in the refrigerator for at least three hours and preferably overnight. The salt in the rub is slowly absorbed by the meat and carries some of the spices with it. The result is a more evenly flavored piece of meat.

Master Recipe

Barbecued Pulled Pork

NOTE: *Preparing pulled pork requires little effort but lots of time. Plan on nine hours from start to finish: three hours covered with the spice rub, three hours on the grill, two hours in the oven, and one hour to rest. Hickory is the traditional choice with pork, although mesquite may be used if desired. Serve the pulled pork on plain white bread or warmed buns with the classic accompaniments of dill pickle chips and cole slaw. Serves eight.*

- ¾ cup Dry Rub for Barbecue (page 92)
- 1 bone-in pork roast, preferably Boston butt (*see* figure 19), 6 to 8 pounds
- 4 3-inch wood chunks or 4 cups wood chips
- Heavy-duty aluminum foil
- Disposable aluminum roasting pan (about 8" x 10")
- Brown paper grocery bag
- 2 cups Barbecue Sauce (page 94)

INSTRUCTIONS:

1. If using fresh ham or picnic roast, remove skin (*see* figure 20). Massage dry rub into meat. Wrap tightly in double layer of plastic wrap and refrigerate for at least 3 hours. (For stronger flavor, roast can be refrigerated for up to 3 days.)

2. About 1 hour prior to cooking, remove roast from refrigerator, and let come to room temperature. Soak wood chunks in cold water to cover for 1 hour and drain, or place wood chips on 18-inch square of aluminum foil, seal to make packet, and use fork to create about six holes to allow smoke to escape (*see* figures 5 and 6, page 19).

3. Meanwhile, light about 40 charcoal briquettes in chimney. Transfer hot coals from chimney to one side of kettle grill, piling them up in a mound two or three briquettes high. Keep bottom vents completely open. When coals are covered with light gray ash, lay wood chunks or packet with chips on top of charcoal. Put cooking grate in place. Set unwrapped roast in disposable pan and place on grate opposite fire (*see* figure 21). Open grill lid vents three-quarters of the way and place lid on grill, turning lid so that vents are opposite wood chunks or chips to draw smoke through grill. Cook, adding about 8 briquettes every hour or so to maintain average temperature of 275 degrees, for 3 hours. Remove from grill and wrap pan holding roast with heavy-duty foil to cover completely.

4. Adjust oven rack to middle position and preheat oven to 325 degrees. Place pan in oven and bake until meat is fork-tender, about 2 hours.

5. Slide foil-wrapped pan with roast into brown bag. Crimp top shut; let roast rest for 1 hour. Transfer roast to cutting board and unwrap. When cool enough to handle, "pull" pork by separating roast into muscle sections (*see* figure 22), removing fat if desired, and tearing meat into thin shreds with fingers (*see* figure 23). Place shredded meat in large bowl; toss with 1 cup barbecue sauce, adding more to taste. Serve with remaining sauce passed separately.

▟ **VARIATION:**

Pulled Pork on a Gas Grill

Follow Pulled Pork Master Recipe, making the following changes: Place foil tray with soaked wood chips (*see* figures 7 through 10, page 23) on top of primary burner (*see* figure 11, page 25). Turn all burners to high and preheat with lid down until chips are smoking heavily, about 20 minutes. Turn primary burner down to medium and turn off burner(s) without chips. Position pan with roast over cool part of grill. Barbecue for 3 hours. (Temperature inside grill should be constant 275 degrees; adjust lit burner as necessary.) Proceed with Master Recipe as directed.

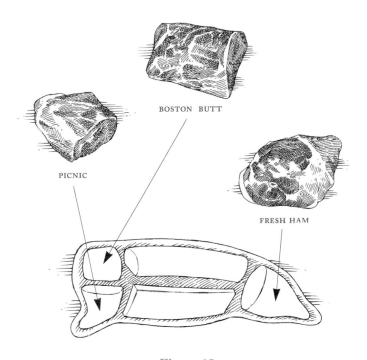

Figure 19.
Although all three cuts make good barbecue, Boston butt is our
first choice because it has enough fat to stay moist and succulent
during the long cooking process.

49

Figure 20.

If using fresh ham or picnic roast (seen here), cut through the skin with the tip of a chef's knife. Slide the knife blade just under the skin and work around to loosen the skin while pulling if off with your other hand. Boston butt does not need to be trimmed.

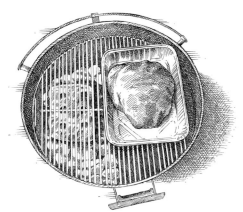

Figure 21.

Set the unwrapped roast, which has been placed in a disposable pan barely larger than the meat itself, on the grill rack opposite the coals and the wood.

5 0

Figure 22.
As soon as the meat is cool enough to handle, remove the meat from
the bones and separate the major muscle sections with your hands.

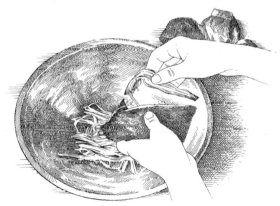

Figure 23.
Remove as much fat as desired and tear the meat into thin strips.

51

chapter five

ᗏ

BARBECUED
SALMON

E WONDERED IF IT WAS POSSIBLE TO
cook a whole side of salmon over low
barbecue heat. Our goal was to produce
a fish perfumed with smoke flavor (like
smoked salmon). However, we wanted to cook the fish (not
just smoke it), making it possible to serve the fish in large
pieces as a main course.

When we first tried cooking a whole side of salmon over
indirect heat, we liked the smoke flavor but felt that the
salmon became too dry during the hour and a half cooking
time. We tried brushing the salmon with oil and then with
a moist sauce, but neither improved the texture of the fish

much below the surface.

At this point, we decided to try brining the salmon. Gravlax (which is cured but not smoked) is brined. Of course, we know from previous experience that brining helps poultry hold onto moisture as it cooks.

We tested a simple salt water brine and felt that it helped the fish retain more moisture as it barbecued. We also tried a brine with salt and sugar and found that the sweetness worked well with the flavor of the fish. As for the timing, we found that the fish benefits most from three hours of brining.

The actual cooking process is ridiculously simple. The fish is placed over indirect heat and cooked just until the thickest part of the fillet will flake. We built a modest charcoal fire with 40 briquettes and found that the salmon was done after an hour and a half. There was no need to add any charcoal as the salmon cooked, making this a quick and easy way to enjoy barbecue flavor.

As with poultry (*see* chapter 6), we found that salmon cooked over charcoal was significantly drier than salmon cooked over gas. Charcoal-barbecued salmon is still delicious and plenty moist (thanks to brining), but the difference is readily apparent.

♛

Master Recipe

Barbecued Salmon

➤ **NOTE:** *Alder wood is our first choice for this recipe, although hickory or mesquite are fine. Make sure the grill grate is hot and thoroughly cleaned before placing the salmon on it; otherwise the fish might stick. This salmon is delicious as is but tastes even better when served with either of the sauces on page 59. Serve the salmon hot, at room temperature, or wrap the cooled fillet in plastic and chill overnight. Serves four to six.*

1	cup kosher salt or ⅔ cup table salt
1	cup sugar
1	skin-on salmon fillet (about 2½ pounds), any pin bones removed with tweezers or needle-nose pliers
2	3-inch wood chunks or 2 cups wood chips Heavy-duty aluminum foil
2	tablespoons vegetable oil
1½	teaspoons sweet paprika
1	teaspoon ground white pepper

▞ **INSTRUCTIONS:**

1. Place salt and sugar in gallon-size zipper-lock plastic bag. Add 2 cups hot water and let stand 20 minutes to let salt and sugar dissolve. Add 5 cups cold water. Place salmon in brine, seal bag, and refrigerate for 3 hours.

2. Soak wood chunks in cold water to cover for 1 hour and drain, or place wood chips on 18-inch square of aluminum foil, seal to make packet, and use fork to create about six holes to allow smoke to escape (*see* figures 5 and 6, page 19).

3. Remove salmon from brine and blot dry completely with paper towels. Place fillet, skin side down, on double layer of foil and rub both sides, especially skin side, with oil. Dust top of fillet with paprika and pepper.

4. Meanwhile, light about 40 charcoal briquettes in chimney. Transfer hot coals from chimney to one side of kettle grill, piling them up in a mound two or three briquettes high. Keep bottom vents completely open. When coals are covered with light gray ash, lay wood chunks or packet with chips on top of charcoal. Put cooking grate in place, open grill lid vents completely and place lid on grill, turning lid so that vents are opposite wood chunks or pouch to draw smoke through grill. Let grate heat for 5 minutes, clean with wire brush, and slide salmon off foil and onto grate opposite fire so that long side of fillet is perpendicular to grill rods (*see* figure 24). (Initial temperature will be about 350 degrees but will drop to about 250 degrees before salmon is done.)

Barbecue for 1½ hours.

5. Using two spatulas (*see* figure 25), remove salmon from grill. To serve, cut through pink flesh but not skin to divide into individual portions (*see* figure 26). Slide spatula between fillet and skin to remove individual pieces, leaving skin behind (*see* figure 27).

▪▪ VARIATION:

Barbecued Salmon on a Gas Grill

Follow Barbecued Salmon Master Recipe, making the following changes: Place foil tray with soaked wood chips (*see* figures 7 through 10, page 23) on top of primary burner (*see* figure 11, page 25). Turn all burners to high and preheat with lid down until chips are smoking heavily, about 20 minutes. Turn primary burner down to medium, turn off burner(s) without chips, and clean grill with wire brush. Position salmon over cool part of grill with long side of fillet perpendicular to grill rods. Barbecue for 1½ hours. (Temperature inside grill should be a constant 275 degrees; adjust lit burner as necessary.) Serve as directed in Master Recipe.

Figure 24.
Slide the salmon off the foil and onto the grill. To make it easier
to remove the salmon from the grill once it is done, position the
fillet so that the long side is perpendicular to the grill rods.

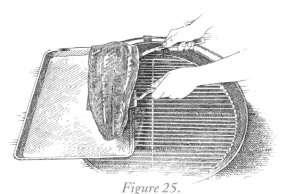

Figure 25.
Use two spatulas to transfer the cooked fish from the grill to a
cookie sheet or cutting board.

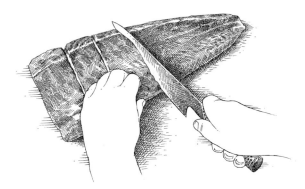

Figure 26.
To serve, cut through the pink flesh, but not the skin, to divide
into individual portions.

Figure 27.
Slide a spatula between the fillet and skin to remove
individual pieces, leaving the skin behind.

Sauces for Barbecued Salmon

➤ NOTE: *Either of these sauces makes a good accompaniment to salmon, adding flavor and moisture to the fish. The horseradish sauce will be a little looser and creamier if made with crème fraîche but is also delicious with sour cream. Dijon, honey, or grainy mustard can be used in the second sauce. Each recipe makes about 1 cup.*

Horseradish Cream Sauce

1   cup crème fraîche or sour cream
2   tablespoons prepared horseradish, or more
    to taste
    Pinch salt

Mustard Dill Sauce

1   cup mustard (*see* note above)
¼   cup minced fresh dill

⏛ INSTRUCTIONS:

Combine ingredients in small bowl. (Can be covered and refrigerated overnight.)

chapter six

GRILL-ROASTED POULTRY

GRILL-ROASTING POULTRY—COOKING IT IN a covered grill over indirect heat at a temperature between 350 and 400 degrees—is an impressive feat. As with a conventionally roasted chicken, we wanted the meat to remain moist and tender while the skin became bronzed and crisp. We also wanted the bird to pick up a good amount of smoke flavor.

We intended to develop recipes for turkey, chicken, and game hens and found that the issues to be decided were pretty much the same for all the birds, with a few important differences.

First of all, we found it imperative to choose a small

turkey (12 to 14 pounds gross weight, 11 to 13 pounds once the giblets have been removed and the turkey drained). Mammoth 18-pound birds won't fit in most grills and are difficult to cook through without burning the skin.

Second, we found it helpful to lift the turkey off the grill rack by placing it in a V-rack. The slight elevation of the V-rack promotes even circulation of heat within the grill. Conversely, we found no benefit to using the V-rack with chickens and hens, which are so small they can sit right on the grill and still get good air circulation. In fact, placing these smaller birds on the grill crisps their skin better during their relatively short cooking time.

Even with Cornish hens, a charcoal fire will die down before the meat is cooked through and the skin crisps. For this reason, we found it necessary to build a relatively large fire and then add more coals halfway through the cooking time. Of course, using a gas grill guarantees a constant source of heat and eliminates this issue.

We conducted several tests to see if turning and basting were necessary. We found that starting the birds breast side down and then turning them halfway through the cooking time kept the breast juicy and was worth the effort. Rotating the birds 180 degrees, so that the opposite side faces the fire, promotes even cooking. With the turkey, we tested two more turns—putting the turkey on either side—

but too much heat was lost from the grill and we had to add even more charcoal. More important, the turkey did not taste any juicier for the extra effort.

As for basting, we found that basting with butter before grilling can speed the browning of the skin on chickens and hens. However, we found that turkeys (which require much longer cooking times) can actually overbrown when basted at the start. Since the grill must be opened to turn the bird, we used that opportunity to baste with butter and had excellent results.

We found that all birds benefit greatly from brining. With the turkey, which is especially prone to drying out, we consider brining mandatory. If you have the time, it's worthwhile to brine chickens and hens before grill-roasting as well.

One final note: We found that birds cooked over charcoal absorb more smoke flavor but were also noticeably drier. (Brining birds destined for charcoal grills mitigates this problem.) Birds cooked over gas were significantly moister but also don't absorb as much smoke. In either case, grill-roasted poultry should be served with some sort of salsa or chutney for added moisture and flavor. Cranberry sauce or relish is also appropriate.

⚜

Master Recipe

Grill-Roasted Turkey

➤ NOTE: *Make sure your grill lid is tall enough to accommodate both your turkey and a V-rack. Brining before grill-roasting improves the flavor and texture of the turkey. If you decide not brine, rub the turkey generously with salt before grilling. Grill-roasted turkey is a great choice for summer entertaining. The usual summer poultry accompaniments—salsa or chutney to moisten the bird, plus potato salad or cole slaw—can replace Thanksgiving standbys like cranberry sauce, stuffing, and mashed potatoes. Serves 10 to 12.*

1   turkey (12 to 14 pounds), rinsed thoroughly, giblets removed, and wing tips tucked behind back (*see* figure 31, page 73)

2   cups kosher salt or 1⅓ cups table salt

3   3-inch wood chunks or 3 cups wood chips and heavy-duty aluminum foil

1   medium onion, coarsely chopped

1   small carrot, coarsely chopped

1   celery stalk, coarsely chopped

3   thyme sprigs

3   tablespoons unsalted butter, melted

⠿ INSTRUCTIONS:

1. To brine turkey: Dissolve salt in 2 gallons of cold water in large stock pot or clean bucket. Add turkey, breast side down, and refrigerate or set in very cool (40 degrees or less) spot for 12 hours.

2. When almost ready to cook, soak wood chunks in cold water to cover for 1 hour and drain, or place wood chips on 18-inch square of aluminum foil, seal to make packet, and use fork to create about six holes to allow smoke to escape (*see* figures 5 and 6, page 19).

3. Remove turkey from salt water and rinse inside and out under cool running water for several minutes until all traces of salt are gone. Pat turkey dry, inside and out, with paper towels. Toss onion, carrot, celery, and thyme with 1 tablespoon melted butter and place mixture in cavity of turkey.

4. Meanwhile, light chimney filled with charcoal briquettes. Transfer hot coals from chimney to one side of kettle grill, piling them up in a mound three briquettes high. Keep bottom vents halfway open. When coals are covered with light gray ash, lay wood chunks or packet with chips on top of charcoal. Put cooking grate in place, position turkey, breast side down, in V-rack, and set V-rack securely on grate opposite fire (*see* figure 28). Open grill lid vents halfway and place lid on grill, turning lid so that vents are opposite wood chunks or chips to draw smoke through grill. (Initial temperature will be about 375 degrees and will drop to about 325 degrees after an hour.) Grill-roast turkey, covered, for about 1 hour.

5. Using thick pot holders, remove V-rack with turkey from grill and place it in large roasting pan. Working as quickly as possible, remove grill rack, move foil packet aside, if using, add 12 more briquettes, stir them into pile, return foil packet, if using, and place grill rack back in position. Baste back side of turkey with melted butter. With wad of paper towels in each hand, turn turkey breast side up in V-rack. Baste breast side of turkey. Return V-rack with turkey to grill so that the side of the turkey that was facing away from the fire now faces the coals. Quickly replace lid and continue grill-roasting until instant-read thermometer inserted into thigh registers between 165 and 170 degrees, 1 to 1¼ hours longer, depending on grill temperature. Remove turkey from the grill, let rest for 20 to 30 minutes, carve, and serve.

∷ VARIATIONS:
Grill-Roasted Turkey on a Gas Grill

Follow Grill-Roasted Turkey Master Recipe, making the following changes: Place foil tray with soaked wood chips (*see* figures 7 through 10, page 23) on top of primary burner (*see* figure 11, page 25). Turn all burners to high and preheat with lid down until chips are smoking heavily, about 20 minutes. Leave primary burner on high and turn off other burner(s). Position turkey in V-rack over cool part of grill. Grill-roast for an hour, turning and basting as directed, and continue to grill-roast until cooked through, 1 to 1¼ hours longer. (Temperature inside grill should average between 350 and 375 degrees; adjust lit burner as necessary.)

Grill-Roasted Turkey with Spice Rub

Follow Grill-Roasted Turkey Master Recipe or gas grill variation, making the following changes: Omit onion, carrot, celery, thyme, and butter. Coat skin with ½ cup of either spice rub on page 93. Grill-roast as directed.

Figure 28.
Place turkey breast side down in a V-rack and set the rack over the cool part of fire.

66

♔

Master Recipe

Grill-Roasted Chicken

➤ NOTE: *Although brining is not essential, it is recommended, especially when cooking over charcoal. Mix 4 quarts water with 1 cup kosher salt or ⅔ cup table salt and refrigerate the bird, breast side down, in this mixture for 6 to 8 hours. Drain and rinse (see turkey recipe on page 63 for details), and omit the salt in step 2 below. Serves four.*

2   3-inch wood chunks or 2 cups wood chips and heavy-duty aluminum foil

1   whole chicken (about 3½ pounds), giblets discarded, chicken rinsed and patted dry with paper towels, and wing tips tucked behind back (*see* figure 31, page 73)

2   tablespoons unsalted butter, melted
     Salt and ground black pepper

▮▮ INSTRUCTIONS:

1. Soak wood chunks in cold water to cover for 1 hour and drain, or place wood chips on 18-inch square of aluminum foil, seal to make packet, and use fork to create about six holes to allow smoke to escape (*see* figures 5 and 6, page 19).

2. Brush chicken, including cavity, with butter, and sprinkle with salt and pepper to taste.

6 7

3. Meanwhile, fill chimney with charcoal briquettes and light. Transfer hot coals from chimney to one side of kettle grill, piling them up in a mound three briquettes high. Keep bottom vents halfway open. When coals are covered with light gray ash, lay wood chunks or packet with chips on top of charcoal. Put cooking grate in place, open grill lid vents halfway and place lid on grill, turning lid so that vents are opposite wood chunks or chips to draw smoke through grill. Let grate heat for 5 minutes, clean with wire brush, and position chicken, breast side down, on grate opposite fire. (Initial temperature will be about 375 degrees.) Grill-roast chicken, covered, for about 30 minutes.

4. Using heavy-duty tongs, remove chicken from grill and place it in large roasting pan. Working as quickly as possible, remove grill rack, push foil packet aside, if using, add 12 more briquettes, stir them into pile, return foil packet, if using, and place grill rack back in position. Return chicken, breast side up, to grill so that side of chicken that was facing away from fire is now facing coals. Quickly replace lid and continue grill-roasting until instant-read thermometer inserted into thigh and breast registers between 165 and 170 degrees, 30 to 40 minutes longer, depending on grill temperature. Remove chicken from grill, let rest for 10 minutes, carve, and serve.

▌▌ **VARIATIONS:**

Grill-Roasted Chicken on a Gas Grill

Follow Grill-Roasted Chicken Master Recipe, making the following changes: Place foil tray with soaked wood chips (*see* figures 7 through 10, page 23) on top of primary burner (*see* figure 11, page 25). Turn all burners to high and preheat with lid down until chips are smoking heavily, about 20 minutes. Leave primary burner on high and turn off other burner. (If using grill with three burners, turn off middle burner and turn others to medium.) Position chicken, breast side down, over cool part of grill. Grill-roast, turning as directed, for 50 to 60 minutes. (Temperature inside grill should be 350 to 375 degrees; adjust lit burner as necessary.)

Grill-Roasted Chicken with Barbecue Sauce

Follow Grill-Roasted Chicken Master Recipe or gas grill variation, brushing chicken with ¼ cup Barbecue Sauce (page 94) during last 10 minutes of cooking. Continue as directed, checking frequently to make sure sauce does not burn.

Grill-Roasted Chicken with Spice Rub

Follow Grill-Roasted Chicken Master Recipe or gas grill variation, omitting butter and coating skin with ¼ cup of either spice rub on page 93. Sprinkle with salt to taste and grill-roast as directed.

69

♛

Master Recipe

Grill-Roasted Cornish Hens

➤ **NOTE:** *Most supermarket game hens have very little flavor and really benefit from brining. Mix 4 quarts water with ¾ cup kosher salt or ½ cup table salt and refrigerate the birds in this mixture for 6 to 8 hours. Drain and rinse (see turkey recipe on page 63 for details), and omit the salt in step 2 below. Either of the chicken flavor variations on page 69 may be adapted to the hens as long as you divide the flavoring mixture evenly between the two birds. Serves four.*

- 2   3-inch wood chunks or 2 cups wood chips and heavy-duty aluminum foil
- 2   Cornish game hens (about 3 pounds total), giblets discarded, hens rinsed and patted dry with paper towels, skin pricked (*see* figure 29), legs tied (*see* figure 30), and wings tucked (*see* figure 31)
- 2   tablespoons unsalted butter, melted
      Salt and ground black pepper

▓ **INSTRUCTIONS:**

1. Soak wood chunks in cold water to cover for 1 hour and drain, or place wood chips on 18-inch square of aluminum foil, seal to make packet, and use fork to create about six holes to allow smoke to escape (*see* figures 5 and 6, page 19).

70

2. Brush hens, including cavity, with butter, and sprinkle with salt and pepper to taste.

3. Meanwhile, fill chimney with charcoal briquettes and light. Transfer hot coals from chimney to one side of kettle grill, piling them up in a mound three briquettes high. Keep bottom vents halfway open. When coals are covered with light gray ash, lay wood chunks or packet with chips on top of charcoal. Put cooking grate in place, open grill lid vents halfway and place lid on grill, turning lid so that vents are opposite wood chunks or chips to draw smoke through grill. Let grate heat for 5 minutes, clean with wire brush, and position hens, breast side down, on grate opposite fire. (Initial temperature will be about 375 degrees.) Grill-roast hens, covered, for about 30 minutes.

4. Using heavy-duty tongs, remove hens from grill and place them in large roasting pan. Working as quickly as possible, remove grill rack, push foil packet aside, if using, add 12 more briquettes, stir them into pile, return foil packet, if using, and place grill rack back in position. Return hens, breast side up, to grill so that sides of hens that were facing away from fire are now facing coals. Quickly replace lid and continue grill-roasting until instant-read thermometer inserted into thigh registers between 165 and 170 degrees, about 30 minutes longer. Remove hens from grill, let rest for 10 minutes, carve, and serve.

▪▪ VARIATION:

Grill-Roasted Cornish Hens on a Gas Grill

Follow Grill-Roasted Cornish Hens Master Recipe, making the following changes: Place foil tray with soaked wood chips (*see* figures 7 through 10, page 23) on top of primary burner (*see* figure 11, page 25). Turn all burners to high and preheat with lid down until chips are smoking heavily, about 20 minutes. Leave primary burner on high and turn off other burner. (If using grill with three burners, turn off middle burner and turn others to medium.) Grill-roast, turning as directed, for 40 to 50 minutes. (Temperature inside grill should be 350 to 375 degrees; adjust lit burner as necessary.)

Figure 29.
To prevent the skin from ballooning when juices build up, carefully prick the skin (but not the meat) on the breast and leg of each Cornish hen with the tip of a knife.

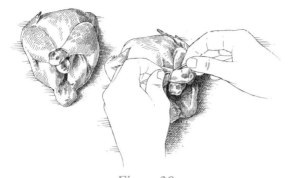

Figure 30.
To keep the legs close to the body and prevent them from burning,
tie the legs of each hen together with a short piece of twine.

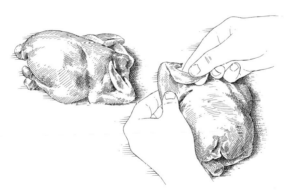

Figure 31.
To keep the wings close to the body and prevent them from
burning or falling off, tuck the wing tips behind the back.

73

chapter seven

GRILL-ROASTED BEEF TENDERLOIN

ECAUSE THE TENDERLOIN SITS UP JUST UNDER the spine of the cow, it gets no exercise at all and is therefore the most tender piece of meat on the animal. It is one of the two muscles on either side of the bone in the ultra-premium steak known as the porterhouse, so when it is removed from the cow as a whole muscle, it sells for an ultra-premium price.

A whole beef tenderloin can be purchased "unpeeled," with an incredibly thick layer of exterior fat left attached, but it's usually sold "peeled," or stripped of its fat. Because of our many bad experiences with overly lean meat, we pur-

74

chased several unpeeled roasts. However, it quickly became clear that there was too much fat to leave on the roast. We found that the fat prevented the formation of a thick brown crust, one of the hallmarks of a perfectly cooked tenderloin.

We then tried peeling the roasts in the test kitchen. In the end we removed three pounds of waste from an eight-pound unpeeled roast, which had cost us $56. Since we could buy a five-pound peeled roast for just $40, the unpeeled roast was actually more expensive per pound of edible meat and required a lot more effort. In fact, we found it best to leave the peeled roast alone, letting the scattered patches of fat on the exterior flavor the meat as it cooked.

Grill-roasting a whole tenderloin poses a challenge because of its shape (*see* figure 32). This cut is thick at one end and tapered at the other, which makes for uneven cooking. The solution to this problem was to fold under the tip end of the roast. We found that tying the roast bulks up the tenderloin center so it is almost as thick as the more substantial butt tender. Tying the roast also ensures even cooking.

As for the actual cooking process, we found that a beef tenderloin cooks perfectly over indirect heat in 35 to 40 minutes. To build a nice thick crust on the meat, the initial charcoal fire should be fairly hot—about 375 degrees is ideal. We tried turning the roast but found that opening the lid caused the fire to lose heat and that the roast was browning evenly anyway.

Once the roast is cooked to 125 degrees (the optimum temperature if you like your meat cooked medium-rare), it should be pulled off the grill and allowed to rest; the internal temperature will rise by at least 5 degrees. Most roasts can be carved after 15 minutes, but we found that beef tenderloin improves dramatically if left uncarved even longer. If cut too soon, the slices are soft and flabby. A slightly longer rest, however, allows the meat to firm up into a more appealing texture.

♛

Master Recipe

Grill-Roasted Beef Tenderloin

➤ NOTE: *There's no advantage to buying an unpeeled tenderloin. It seems cheaper, but we found that once the fat is trimmed away you don't save any money. If you can't find a whole tenderloin with the tip end (see figure 32) attached, use a smaller tenderloin and omit the tucking step. The cooking time will be about the same for the smaller roast because it is just as thick. The tenderloin can be served as is or with a double recipe of Horseradish Cream Sauce (page 59). A whole tenderloin serves 10 to 12.*

1 whole peeled beef tenderloin (about 5 pounds), thoroughly patted dry, silver skin cut (*see* figure 33), tip end tucked under (*see* figure 34), and tied (*see* figure 35)

2 3-inch wood chunks or 2 cups wood chips and heavy-duty aluminum foil

2 tablespoons olive oil

1 tablespoon kosher salt or 2 teaspoons table salt

2 tablespoons coarse-ground black pepper

INSTRUCTIONS:

1. An hour before cooking, remove roast from refrigerator to bring it to room temperature.

2. Soak wood chunks in cold water to cover for 1 hour and drain, or place wood chips on 18-inch square of aluminum foil, seal to make packet, and use fork to create about six holes to allow smoke to escape (*see* figures 5 and 6, page 19).

3. Set roast on sheet of plastic wrap and rub all over with oil. Sprinkle with salt and pepper and then lift wrap to press on excess (*see* figure 36, page 83).

4. Meanwhile, light chimney filled with charcoal briquettes. Transfer hot coals from chimney to one side of kettle grill, piling them up in a mound three briquettes high. Keep bottom vents completely open. When coals are covered with light gray ash, lay wood chunks or packet with chips on top of charcoal. Put cooking grate in place, open grill lid vents completely and place lid on grill, turning lid so that vents are opposite wood chunks or chips to draw smoke through grill. Let grate heat for 5 minutes, clean with wire brush, and roll tenderloin off plastic and onto grate opposite fire so that long side of fillet is perpendicular to grill rods. (Meat should be positioned like the salmon in figure 24, page 57.) Initial temperature will be about 375 degrees. Grill-roast tenderloin, covered, until instant-read thermometer inserted into thickest part of roast registers about 125 degrees, 35 to 40 minutes.

5. Let stand about 30 minutes before carving. Cut roast into slices ½-inch thick and serve. (Whole roast can be wrapped in plastic, refrigerated up to 2 days, sliced, and served chilled.)

▪▪ VARIATIONS:

Grill-Roasted Beef Tenderloin on a Gas Grill

Follow Grill-Roasted Beef Tenderloin Master Recipe, making the following changes: Place foil tray with soaked wood chips (*see* figures 7 through 10, page 23) on top of primary burner (*see* figure 11, page 25). Turn all burners to high and preheat with lid down until chips are smoking heavily, about 20 minutes. Leave primary burner on high and turn off other burner. (If using grill with three burners, turn off middle burner and leave others on high.) Position tenderloin over cool part of grill. Grill-roast for 30 to 35 minutes. (Temperature inside grill should average between 375 to 400 degrees; adjust lit burner as necessary.)

Grill-Roasted Beef Tenderloin with Pepper Crust

Follow Grill-Roasted Beef Tenderloin Master Recipe or gas grill variation, increase pepper to 6 tablespoons, and use mixture of strong white and black as well as mild pink and green peppercorns. Coarsely crush peppercorns with mortar and pestle or with heavy saucepan or skillet.

Grill-Roasted Beef Tenderloin with Garlic and Rosemary

Studding the tenderloin with slivered garlic and fresh rosemary gives it an Italian flavor.

Follow Grill-Roasted Beef Tenderloin Master Recipe or gas grill variation, making following changes: After tying roast, use paring knife to make several dozen shallow incisions around surface of roast. Stuff a few fresh rosemary needles and 1 thin sliver of garlic into each incision. (A total of 1 tablespoon rosemary and 3 large garlic cloves, slivered.) Oil as directed. Sprinkle with salt, pepper, and additional 2 tablespoons minced rosemary. Proceed as directed.

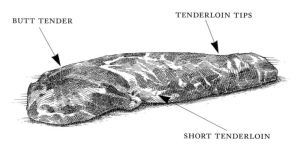

BUTT TENDER

TENDERLOIN TIPS

SHORT TENDERLOIN

Figure 32.
A whole beef tenderloin comprises three sections: The thicker end of the roast is called the butt tender, and the middle portion—virtually an even thickness—is called the short tenderloin; the tapering tip end is sold as part of the whole tenderloin or removed and sold as tenderloin tips.

80

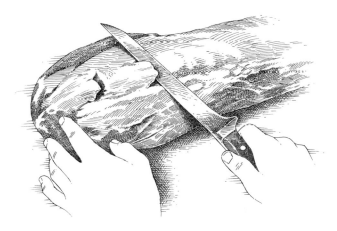

Figure 33.
To keep the meat from bowing as it cooks, slide a knife under the
silver skin and flick the blade upward to cut through the silver
skin at five or six spots along the length of the roast.

81

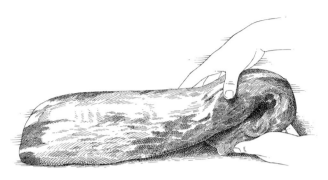

Figure 34.
To ensure that the tenderloin roasts more evenly, fold the thin tip end of the roast under about 6 inches.

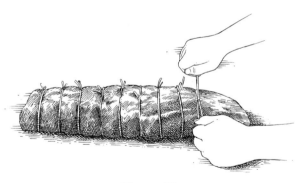

Figure 35.
For more even cooking and evenly sized slices, use 12-inch lengths of kitchen twine to tie the roast every 1½ inches.

82

Figure 36.
Set the roast on a sheet of plastic wrap and rub it all over with
oil. Sprinkle with salt and pepper, then lift the plastic wrap up
and around the meat to press on the excess. This method
guarantees even coverage of the roast and can be used with
the pepper crust or a spice rub.

chapter eight

GRILL-ROASTED PORK LOIN

A BONELESS PORK ROAST IS AN IDEAL CANDI-
date for grill-roasting. As opposed to barbecued pulled pork, which starts out with a very
fatty cut from the shoulder or leg, lean loin
roasts are the best choice for relatively quick grill-roasting
since they are already tender. However, unlike the thin tenderloin, the loin is too thick to cook over direct heat. The exterior chars long before the interior comes up to temperature.

The pork loin runs along one side of the backbone of the
pig, starting at the shoulder, or blade bone, and ending at
the hip bone. For roasting (whether on the grill or in the
oven), we found that the meat from the center of the loin,

called the center loin roast or center-cut loin roast, is best. This piece of meat contains a single muscle, so the grain is tender and easy to carve. The center loin roast is a fairly pale piece of meat and has a relatively mild flavor.

We cooked the two other boneless roasts from the loin before deciding to go with the center loin roast. The blade roast, also called the blade loin roast or loin roast, contains small parts of various shoulder muscles that are redder and more fibrous than the center loin. The meat at the other end of the loin, which is called rib end, hip end, or sirloin roast, is also more fibrous and tougher than the center loin.

Unlike a beef tenderloin, a pork center loin has a fairly even thickness from end to end so there is no need to tuck up one side or the other. To make the meat perfectly even and ensure proper cooking, we found it helpful to tie the roast at regular intervals.

A pork loin can be grill-roasted much like a beef tenderloin. The biggest challenge is keeping the meat moist. A beef tenderloin can be pulled from the grill when the internal temperature reaches 125 degrees and eaten medium-rare. Pork must be cooked to a higher internal temperature to make the meat palatable (rare pork has an unappealing texture) and to kill any possible parasites.

After testing various temperatures, we found that the center loin roast should be pulled from the grill when the internal temperature registers 145 degrees on an instant-read thermometer. After the meat rests for 20 minutes, the temperature will rise to about 155 degrees. The meat will have a slight tinge of pink, but it will be far juicier than roasts cooked to an internal temperature that is just 10 degrees higher. (A temperature of 155 degrees is high enough to kill the parasite that causes trichinosis. However, the USDA recommends cooking all meat to an internal temperature of 160 degrees to kill bacteria such as salmonella. If safety is your primary concern, follow the USDA's guidelines.)

While we had little trouble getting the meat properly cooked on the grill (as with the beef tenderloin, there is no need to turn the meat as it cooks), we found the roast to be a bit bland and not as moist as we might have liked. Both problems stem from the fact that most of the internal fat has been bred out of the pig in recent years. We hit upon two strategies for making the meat taste better and juicier when cooked.

If you have the time, pork (like lean poultry) responds well to brining. A brined pork roasts up juicier, and the salt-water bath also flavors the meat nicely. Our second solution for boosting the flavor in pork loin is to season it aggressively. A potent spice rub or a heady mixture of garlic and rosemary will dramatically improve the flavor of the meat.

Master Recipe

Grill-Roasted Pork Loin

➤ **NOTE:** *Make sure to buy the center loin roast. Do not buy rib end, blade end, or loin end roasts, which have many muscle separations and can be quite tough. The entire center loin weighs 6 to 9 pounds when boned. It is commonly sold in smaller pieces, which usually weigh 3 or 4 pounds. If possible, we strongly recommend that you brine the meat in a mixture of 4 quarts cold water and 1 cup kosher salt or ⅔ cup table salt for 8 hours. Brining makes the meat considerably more moist and flavorful. If brining, omit the salt in step 3. Moisten the roast with salsa, chutney, or even applesauce. Serves 8 to 10.*

1	boneless center loin roast (about 4 pounds), tied (*see* figure 35, page 82)
2	3-inch wood chunks or 2 cups wood chips and heavy-duty aluminum foil
2	tablespoons olive oil
1	tablespoon kosher salt or 2 teaspoons table salt
2	tablespoons coarse-ground black pepper

INSTRUCTIONS:

1. An hour before cooking, remove roast from refrigerator to bring it to room temperature.

2. Soak wood chunks in cold water to cover for 1 hour and drain, or place wood chips on 18-inch square of aluminum foil, seal to make packet, and use fork to create about six holes to allow smoke to escape (*see* figures 5 and 6, page 19).

3. Set roast on sheet of plastic wrap and rub all over with oil. Sprinkle with salt and pepper and then lift wrap to press on excess (*see* figure 36, page 83).

4. Meanwhile, light chimney filled with charcoal briquettes. Transfer hot coals from chimney to one side of kettle grill, piling them up in a mound three briquettes high. Keep bottom vents completely open. When coals are covered with light gray ash, lay wood chunks or packet with chips on top of charcoal. Put cooking grate in place, open grill lid vents completely and place lid on grill, turning lid so that vents are opposite wood chunks or chips to draw smoke through grill. Let grate heat for 5 minutes, clean with wire brush, and roll pork loin off plastic and onto grate opposite fire so that long side of fillet is perpendicular to grill rods. (Meat should be positioned the same way as the salmon in figure 24, page 57.) Initial temperature will be about 375 degrees. Grill-roast pork loin, covered, until instant-read thermometer inserted into thickest part of roast registers about 145 degrees, 40 to 50 minutes.

5. Let stand about 20 minutes before carving. Internal temperature should register between 150 and 155 degrees. (Can

8 8

be wrapped in plastic and refrigerated up to 2 days.) Cut roast into slices ½-inch thick and serve.

░░ VARIATIONS:

Grill-Roasted Pork Loin on a Gas Grill

Follow Grill-Roasted Pork Loin Master Recipe, making the following changes: Place foil tray with soaked wood chips (*see* figures 7 through 10, page 23) on top of primary burner (*see* figure 11, page 25). Turn all burners to high and preheat with lid down until chips are smoking heavily, about 20 minutes. Leave primary burner on high and turn off other burner. (If using grill with three burners, turn off middle burner and leave others on high.) Position loin over cool part of grill. Grill-roast for 35 to 45 minutes. (Temperature inside grill should average between 375 to 400 degrees; adjust lit burner as necessary.)

Grill-Roasted Pork Loin with Garlic and Rosemary

Follow Grill-Roasted Pork Loin Master Recipe or gas grill variation, making following changes: After tying roast, use paring knife to make several dozen shallow incisions around surface of roast. Stuff a few fresh rosemary needles and 1 thin sliver of garlic into each incision. (You will need a total of 1 tablespoon rosemary and 3 large garlic cloves, slivered.) Oil as directed. Sprinkle with salt, pepper, and additional 2 tablespoons rosemary. Proceed as directed.

chapter nine

RUBS & SAUCES

UBBED ONTO THE OUTSIDE OF FOODS, SPICE blends encourage the formation of a deeply browned crust filled with complex, concentrated flavors. Like marinades, spice rubs add flavor to foods, but they have several advantages over their wet counterparts.

Since they are composed almost solely of spices, they provide stronger flavors than marinades, which typically contain oil, an acidic liquid, and spices. Rubs also stick better to the surface of foods than marinades, which, again, gives them an edge when it comes to intensifying flavor. Finally, marinades almost always contain oil and cause

90

flare-ups on the grill. Spice rubs are ideal for foods that will be barbecued or grill-roasted since they can be left on foods for many hours without causing fires.

We find that bare hands—not brushes—are the best tools for applying spice rubs. Use a bit of pressure to make sure the spices actually adhere to the food. Although rubs can be applied right before cooking, we found that the flavor of the spices penetrates deeper into the food if given some time. In general, we like to refrigerate rubbed meats for a few hours to allow the flavors to develop.

In our tests, we found that the spices continue to penetrate and flavor the meat up until a certain point, beyond which we detect no increase in flavor. We found that the point at which the spice flavor stopped increasing was related to the thickness of the meat. For instance, ribs don't gain any more flavor after spending a day covered with a spice rub. However, a thicker pork roast can be rubbed three days before cooking for maximum spice penetration.

Barbecue sauce is best added to grilled foods at the table. When we added the sauce earlier, we found that the sugars and fat in most sauces caused foods to burn. You may brush barbecue sauce on some foods during the final minutes of grill-roasting, if you like. For instance, you may want to glaze a chicken with sauce, applying it during the last 10 minutes of grill time to set the sauce as a light crust.

9 1

Dry Rub for Barbecue

➤ NOTE: *You may adjust the proportions of spices in this all-purpose rub or add or subtract a spice, as you wish. For instance, if you don't like spicy foods, reduce or eliminate the cayenne. Also, if you are using hot chili powder, you may want to eliminate the cayenne. Makes about 1 cup, enough to coat two full slabs of ribs, one whole brisket, or one Boston butt roast.*

4	tablespoons sweet paprika
2	tablespoons chili powder
2	tablespoons ground cumin
2	tablespoons dark brown sugar
2	tablespoons salt
1	tablespoon dried oregano
1	tablespoon granulated sugar
1	tablespoon ground black pepper
1	tablespoon ground white pepper
1-2	teaspoons cayenne pepper

▪▪ INSTRUCTIONS:

Mix all ingredients in small bowl. (Can be stored in airtight container for several weeks.)

Spice Rubs for Poultry

➤ NOTE: *These rubs are not as potent or peppery as the dry rub for barbecue, making them well suited to mild poultry. Each recipe makes about ½ cup, enough for one turkey. Recipes should be halved for use on one chicken or two Cornish hens.*

Aromatic Rub

1½	tablespoons ground cardamom
1½	tablespoons ground ginger
1½	tablespoons ground black pepper
1	tablespoon ground turmeric
1	tablespoon ground cumin
1	tablespoon ground coriander
1½	teaspoons ground allspice
½	teaspoon ground cloves

Indian Spice Rub

3	tablespoons curry powder
3	tablespoons chili powder
1½	tablespoons ground allspice
1½	teaspoons ground cinnamon

▪▪ INSTRUCTIONS:

Mix ingredients in small bowl. (Can be stored in airtight container for several weeks.)

☙

Master Recipe

Basic Barbecue Sauce

➤ NOTE: *Because barbecue sauce contains so many ingredients that can cause flare-ups on the grill (oil, tomatoes, liquid sweeteners), it should be brushed on foods at the very end of the grilling time or used as dipping sauce at the table. Makes about 3 cups.*

2	tablespoons vegetable oil
1	medium onion, minced
1	cup tomato sauce
1	28-ounce can whole tomatoes with their juice
¾	cup distilled white vinegar
¼	cup packed dark brown sugar
2	tablespoons molasses
1	tablespoon sweet paprika
1	tablespoon chili powder
2	teaspoons liquid smoke (optional)
1	teaspoon salt
2	teaspoons ground black pepper
¼	cup orange juice

▦ INSTRUCTIONS:

1. Heat oil in large, heavy-bottomed saucepan over medium heat. Add onion and sauté until golden brown, 7 to 10 minutes. Add remaining ingredients. Bring to boil, reduce heat to lowest possible setting, and simmer, uncovered, until thickened, 2 to 2½ hours. Cool slightly.

2. Purée sauce, in batches if necessary, in blender or workbowl of food processor. (Sauce can be refrigerated in airtight container for up to 2 weeks.)

▦ VARIATIONS:

Barbecue Sauce with Mexican Flavors
This sauce is good with beef or chicken.

To completed and cooled sauce, add 1½ teaspoons ground cumin, 1½ teaspoons chili powder, 6 tablespoons lime juice, and 3 tablespoons chopped fresh cilantro leaves.

Barbecue Sauce with Asian Flavors
This variation is especially good with chicken or pork.

To completed and cooled sauce, add 1 tablespoon minced fresh gingerroot, 6 tablespoons soy sauce, 6 tablespoons rice wine vinegar, 3 tablespoons sugar, and 1½ tablespoons Asian sesame oil.

index